Osvaldo Golijov

ZZ's Dream

Solo Piano

HENDON MUSIC

7777 W. BLUEMOUND RD. P.O. BOX 13819 MILWAUKEE, WI 53213

www.boosey.com
www.halleonard.com

Published by Hendon Music, Inc.,
a Boosey & Hawkes company
229 West 28th Street, 11th Fl
New York NY 10001

www.boosey.com

First printed 2008
Second printing 2009

ZZ's Dream

Once upon a time, I, Zhuang Zhou, dreamt I was a butterfly, fluttering hither and thither.
I was conscious only of my happiness as a butterfly, unaware that I was Zhou.
Soon I awoke, and there I was, veritably myself again.
Now I do not know whether I was then a man dreaming I was a butterfly,
or whether I am now a butterfly, dreaming I am a man.

Osvaldo Golijov